Durham Priory Kitchen

FROM THE DEAN OF DURHAM
The Very Reverend John Arnold

Tel (0191) 384 7500
Fax (0191) 386 4267

THE DEANERY
DURHAM
DH1 3EQ

In *The Story of The Deanery, Durham* published in 1912 my predecessor Dean Kitchen wrote of 'that remarkable structure of a monastic kitchen undertaken by the Convent, under the guidance of the most vigorous hand of Prior John Fosser. This I believe quite unique in two ways; first because of the excellence of the design and secondly because it is the only early monastic kitchen in England still in regular use.' He is still right in the first of his two reasons; in the second he has been overtaken by the times.

We are therefore doubly indebted to Margot Johnson, not only for bringing all that is usefully known about Durham Priory Kitchen together in a single monograph but also for bringing the story up to date.

I am happy to commend her work for its description of this curious and beautiful building and also for the social and ecclesiastical history which it conveys for the benefit both of the scholar and also of the general reader.

John Arnold.

A. The Building

As part of much rebuilding and expansion in Durham Priory, the Great Kitchen was begun in 1366 in the time of Prior John Fossor (1341-74),[1] to replace an earlier kitchen a little further east, whose foundations may have been uncovered in 1948-9 during the creation of the Durham Light Infantry Memorial Garden.[2] Building continued until 1374, when it was almost completed. Other work was undertaken in the time of Bishop Thomas Langley (1404-67) who contributed £180 18s 7d [£180 93p] to the cost of construction.[3] It is often described as being comparable with a famous medieval kitchen at Fontevrault, in Normandy. The design has no known parallel in the period when it was built,[4] and was either inspired by the tenth-century Muslim work in Spain in the mosque at Cordova or was the invention of the gifted and influential John Lewyn or Lewyne, who flourished 1364-c.1398.[5] At the same time he had in hand the repair of Bamburgh Castle for the Crown, and work for Bishop Thomas Hatfield, perhaps to rebuild the keep of Durham Castle. He was responsible for the building of part of the Durham cloisters, and probably the throne above Bishop Hatfield's tomb in the Cathedral. He had contracts also for work on the castles of Carlisle, Roxburgh, Bolton (*Yorkshire*), Raby, Sheriff Hutton, Wressle, Dunstanburgh, Warkworth, Brancepeth, Finchale Priory, and for the Crown at Berwick-on-Tweed. He was an important Durham citizen, owned several country properties, and was a very large scale wool exporter.

Part of the account for building the Great Kitchen is the earliest fabric roll for any part of the Cathedral and Priory. The roll, closely written in Latin, is five and a quarter yards [9.5256 metres] in length, and has an endorsement two and a half yards [2.286 metres] long. It calls the building the *'new kitchen'*,[6] begins at Martinmas,[7] 1366, and finishes a year and a half later. During this period the monks John de Berrington and later John de Billesfield superintended the work. John Lewyn, the master mason or architect, received 66s. 8d. [£3.33 1/2p] each quarter and a garment worth 13s.4d. [66.5p]. The work over this period cost £180.17s.7d. [£180.88p]; but an expenditure of over £440 is recorded, and the total cost was probably between five hundred and six hundred pounds. The names of the masons, quarrymen, labourers and others are all mentioned weekly. Masons' wages ranged from 3s.8d. [18.5p] to 1s. [5p] per week; quarrymen and labourers were paid 3d. [1p] per day; paviours of the ways through which the materials were carried had 4d. [4.5p] per day. There is an occasional (extra) charge for drink (*ad potum*). The cost for working thirty stones [190.512 kg] of iron into twenty-three masons' axes, twenty-five 'ponsones',[8] with 'chissils', four 'bakkis', two 'pikkis', and nineteen 'weggis', at 4d. [1.5p] per stone [.4536 kgs] was ten shillings [50p]. For working four and half stones [28.5768 kgm] into steel (*in calibem*), for making and repairing the said axes, 'ponsones, chissels, pikkis, and kevellis', and also for working four stones [25.4016 kgs] into a gavelock,[9] the cost was two shillings [10p.]. The price for sharpening 1800 masons' axes (*secur' cementar'*), at 1ld. [4.5p.] per hundred, 16s. 6d. [82.5p.]. A lock for the mason's house was 2d. [1p.].

Most of the workmen have old Durham names, but a few seem to have come from distant places: John de Lincoln, William de Selby, William de Andirstowe, Richard de Goldisburgh, John de Lyndesay,

---

[1] *Historiae Dunelmensis Scriptores Tres, Gaufridus de Coldingham, Robertus de Graystanes, et Willelmus de Chambre* [edited by James Raine], Surtees Society 9 (1839), 132, note.

[2] Friends of Durham Cathedral, *Annual Report 1948-9,* 12-13. The Durham Light Infantry Memorial Garden was dedicated in July 1950.

[3] *Hist. Dunelm. Scriptores Tres,* 146.

[4] Nikolaus Pevsner, *County Durham*. Revised by Elizabeth Williamson (The Buildings of England), 1983, 31: 'one of the most interesting medieval kitchens in Europe'.

[5] John Harvey, *English Medieval Architects ... to 1560*. Second edition, 1994.

[6] The new kitchen was to replace an older building a little to the east.

[7] The feast of St Martin falls on 11 November, and was kept as a Scottish quarter-day.

[8] *ponsones*: mason's punches.

[9] *gavelock*: an iron crowbar or lever.

3

John de Stokesley, John de Benyngbrugh, Robert de Walden, John de Rippon, John de Neddirton from Hertylpoll, Robert de Gisburgh, William de Harwode, Alexander de Ebor, Henry de Ebor, Robert de Esteby, and John de Lethom.[10] Some of these men were fed by the Priory, for we have the entry: 'in meat bought from the Cellarer for workmen having their meals in the small house of the Bursar, and in the neighbourhood, 4s.10d. [24p.]'. The Bursar's exchequer or office between the Kitchen and the Prior's Lodging was built, together with a new larder next the Kitchen, before 1371 for £13.0s.3d. [£13.1p].[11]

The plan

The Great Kitchen survives much as was built, except for two decorated windows which it once possessed, and some small alterations. The basic plan is octagonal, the interior being thirty-six feet [10.9728 metres] in diameter; the added corners, which give a square appearance to the exterior, forming rooms for storage and other purposes. The Cellarer's roll for 1481 mentions the flesh larder, the fish larder, a storehouse, and a slaughter house, which lay east of the kitchen.[12]

Ceiling of the Dean's Kitchen. *R.W.Billings: Architectural Illustrations and Description of the Cathedral Church at Durham (1843)*

[10] James Raine, *A Brief Account of Durham Cathedral* ...(1833), 114-5.
[11] *Extracts from the Account Rolls of the Abbey of Durham, from the original mss*; edited by J.T. Fowler, Surtees Society 99, 100, 103 (1898-1901), 577.
[12] *Victoria History of the County of Durham*, III (1908), 128b.

The impressive and lofty stone vaulted roof[13] has eight semi-circular ribs, each extending over three sides of the octagon.[14] They intersect to form a stellar vault, leaving a central octagonal lantern or opening, fourteen feet in diameter[15] for the louvre which provided ventilation. This net-vaulting resembles examples such as the vault of the mosque at Cordova. The upper face of the vaulting is the outer roof, with no intervening timbers, so that the building is virtually fireproof. The central opening was surmounted originally by a tall structure with its own vaulting and probably with louvered apertures for ventilation on each side, shown in a drawing made by the antiquarian William Stukeley on 12 September 1725, now in the Bodleian Library, Oxford. (The Cellarer's Roll for 1507-8 records new windows here.)

This was replaced in the eighteenth century by a lower gabled louvre, and in 1970 by a reproduction, which may be seen from the College (Cathedral Close) on the south side.

'A Section of the Prior's Kitchin [*sic*], 1911.'

William Stukeley

Roof of Monastic Kitchen, 1911.

W.G. Footitt

The 18th-century lowered gabled louvre.

C.W. Gibby

Originally there were six fireplaces, with flues carried up in the thickness of the walls to chimneys behind the roof parapet. On each wall of the octagon is a relieving arch to carry the weight of the wall above, and each fireplace has its own arch to give added strength over the opening. The three fireplaces on the north side have been adapted: the two to the east to accommodate cooking ranges in the eighteenth and nineteenth centuries. Over one of these are the remains of a smoke-jack, a device for using the rising draught of the flue to turn a spit before the fire for roasting meat. Most of the spits and iron gear survived until at least the 1940s. The third fireplace had been converted into a close-room or curing

---

[13] Raine refers to an engraving by Sir John Hall to support his theory that the interbranching of trees was the inspiration of the arch with its various combinations.

[14] R.W. Billings, *Architectural illustrations and description of the Cathedral Church at Durham* (1843), 50.

[15] *Victoria History of the County of Durham,* III (1908), 148a.

room for curing hams and bacon, but since the 1950s has housed the heating installation. The three fireplaces on the south side have been little altered; .but the central one had an oblong iron pot or receptacle for boiling whole fishes, with a small fireplace beneath it, which could still be used in 1912. At the south-west is an oven with a stone beehive roof, of uncertain date, but shown on a nineteenth-century plan. Another oven is shown behind the fireplace on the north-west wall. One of these may be the one described as a charcoal oven, which could be used for cooking special dishes. Such ovens could also be heated by brushwood burnt inside, and swept out when the stones were hot enough for baking. Bread was inserted on a pele, or long-handled wooden shovel as otherwise the baker could not stand the heat. In monastic times bread was baked in a separate bakehouse. Probably this oven was used for bread in post-monastic times.

Communion bread was not baked in the kitchen but on the west side of the south transept of the Cathedral in a small charcoal-fired oven using obley irons.

Oven with stone 'bee-hive' roof.   *Janet Thackray*

Natural light floods in from two lancet windows high in the south wall, on either side of the flue from the fireplace beneath, where the pitch of the vault above is steeper to accommodate them. They were altered by Dean Spencer Cowper about 1752 when their height was lowered by making a new outer face to the wall, reducing the openings by creating sloping sills, and blocking the tops with false arches of brick covered with plaster which were renewed in stone in 1969-70, when the outside facing was keyed in to the main fabric for the first time.

The main outside entrance to the Kitchen seems originally to have been through the central archway on the east side, which today leads into a comparatively late two-storey addition, replacing an earlier building whose roof line may be seen outside.

This building gave access to two serving hatches, or dresser windows,[16] one still in existence, opening from the monastic frater or refectory which lies alongside the south cloister. These had dressers or

---

[16] *Rites of Durham* ... [edited by J.T. Fowler] Surtees Society 107, Durham (1903), 269. The rough blocked opening of the second serving hatch was found in 1961; *see* Margot Johnson, 'Recent work on the Refectory of Durham Cathedral', in *Transactions of the Architectural and Archaeological Society of Durham and Northumberland*, New Series, Volume 1 (1968), 89.

6

Dresser Hatch to Refectory. *Janet Thackray*

tables on both sides to facilitate the passing through of dishes. One was larger than the other and was opened probably only on more important occasions, such as when the whole convent ate together on the feast of St Cuthbert on 20 March,[17] and on other special days. The smaller hatch was used on a daily basis. Both had heavy double doors opening inwards to the kitchen area.

Nearby was the entrance to the Pentice, an open roofed passage on the south side of the Refectory. It was built in 1340/41 for £6.5s.4d. [£6.26 1/2p/] to connect the kitchen with the Prior's lodging (now the Deanery.[18] Items recur in the monastic Bursar's accounts, with measurements and references to its reconstruction to adapt it to the new Great Kitchen. In early times the Prior ate at the high table on the dais at the east end of the refectory on state occasions, but in later times meals were carried along this passage to be served to him in his own lodgings.

Meals served to the Loft or Gallery, and the Solarium Caritatis

The present narrow entrance to the Great Kitchen on the north-east side replaces a staircase leading to first floor level in the adjacent building. This is shown by the sloping roof of the passage outside the door, and the blocked arch in the library search room above. The staircase led from the Great Kitchen to the loft[19] or gallery above the screens passage at the west end of the refectory (or frater), and the *solarium caritatis* where aged or infirm monks were allowed to eat meat. The whole convent still dined in the refectory itself in 1395, but a Statute of 1444 strictly forbade any but growing youths to dine in the frater from 13 September to Ash Wednesday except on Sundays and festivals.[20] This meant that in late medieval times the loft or gallery became the dining room of the whole convent on ordinary occasions except for the novices, who continued to eat with their master always in the refectory. Their table had a screen of wainscot above it. The older monks entered the loft or gallery by a staircase to the east of the Norman entrance steps which turned westwards against the refectory's north wall.

---

[17] *Rites ...* 4, 79.
[18] Friends of Durham Cathedral, *Sixteenth Annual Report, 1948-9*, T.R[omans], 'The D.L.I. Garden [report of the excavation with photographs], 12-15.
[19] *Rites ...* 86.
[20] *Rites ...* 260, 268.

View of Durham Cathedral: with coal yard and passage from the Great Kitchen to the Prior's Hall.   *H.S. Storer*

The later *solarium caritatis* was probably between the refectory loft and the dormitory. Beneath this room (now the librarian's office) is the small cellar, measuring about 28 feet [8.53 metres] by 10 feet [3.048 metres] internally. A staircase in the north-west corner connected the cellar with the room above. A square opening in the centre of the vault allowed for drawing up and letting down containers of food. Beside the door leading to the cellar from the covey or pantry was a little door, with fastenings, for serving drink from the cellar to the covey without opening the great door.[21]

The Prior's games at Beaurepaire

The monks and novices had an annual outing, when they walked out to the Prior's house at Beaurepaire (Bearpark), taking with them their food with tin plates and mugs. Although the normal day for cleaning the kitchen was Good Friday, a fast day, was this another opportunity for the kitchen staff to let out the fires, clean the kitchen and lime wash the walls?

---

[21] *Rites ... 268.*

8

The Refectory, now the old library: with medieval trestle tables and benches of 1489-1509. *Roger Harris*

Furniture

Some of the furniture survives in the refectory (now the old library): two medieval refectory trestle-tables and benches dated 1485-1509 (probably from the prior's lodgings); and a massive Durham medieval kitchen-table with cupboards is an admired exhibit in the Burrell Collection in Glasgow.

The Cellarer

The different departments of the monastery were each in the charge of an obedientiary (a senior monk), each of whom kept a detailed weekly account. At Durham these were the Sacrist, the Bursar, the Terrar or Hostillar, the Almoner, the Master of the Infirmary, the Master of the Common House, the Chamberlain, and the Cellarer. Each was assisted by servants who wore the livery or uniform of the house.

The Cellarer, one of the few officers named in the Benedictine Rule, was in charge of the food and drink, and arranged for the proper serving of meals. He supervised the monastic mills, the brewhouse, bakehouse, and gardens. As his duties sometimes took him outside the precincts, he was assisted by a sub-cellarer, valecti (upper servants), and grooms (lower servants and yeomen of the kitchen). Chapter 35 of the Benedictine Rule sets out the responsibilities for shared duties and cleanliness in the kitchen. The cook, an upper servant, had a groom under him, and we hear also of the cook of the lord Prior. There were duties also in the Priory at large. Two of the four bells in the Galilee belfry were rung by servants of the

Part of a Durham Priory cresset. *Jean Thornton*

Cellarer: two men from the kitchen rang one bell; and the great bell was rung by two from the bakehouse, two from the brewhouse, and two from the [malt] kiln. The cook supplied fat for the cressets: square stones each with a set of small basins, twelve, eight or six, hollowed out to contain tallow fat and wicks which could be burnt for lighting. Two cressets stood in the dormitory, one at each end of the central passage between the cells, and there was another by the south pillar of the choir door so that the monks could see to enter for their night offices.

Double doors on the west side of the Kitchen (locked by the sub-prior every night)[22] led to the building which contained on its upper floor, with its four south-facing windows, the Cellarer's offices or exchequer, reached by a long flight of stairs.[23] He controlled the purchase of food and drink and kept his stores in the great cellar (now the restaurant) under the south end of the dormitory. The ground floor of the exchequer building was divided by an east - west wall, angled to the south at the east end to accommodate the double doors from the kitchen. Each part was covered by a wagon-vault running east to west. From the north end there was access to the Guest Hall and the Infirmary, and in the north-west corner a door led into the great cellar beneath the dormitory where the bulk of the stores was kept. Each part had two west windows. The south end of the ground floor was used as a stable, at least in later times. In the north-west wall of the Great Kitchen are traces of a doorway and a small blocked window immediately above it, where a staircase in the thickness of the wall probably led to the cellarer's upper floor; and in the same position on the wall outside are traces of an opening at first floor height.

The Cellarer's Roll for 1481 has an inventory of equipment and food in stock.

The Cellarer's checker.
W. Pearson, c.1820.

For the kitchen: 51 platters, 36 dishes, 38 salt-cellars, 9 chargers or large dishes of electrum (a type of brass), 260 platters of wood, 218 dishes of wood, one brass mortar with two iron pestles (to 'bray the spices'), 2 stone mortars with 3 wood pestles, one great brandreth, one small brandreth,[24] 3 pairs of racks, two pairs of cob-irons, two roast irons, 8 long iron-spits, 3 smaller spits, 13 big brass plates, 2 brass chafing dishes, 2 large jars fixed in the fire, 2 large jars for the cooking of meat, 8 brass jars, 5 iron pots to boil things in, 3 vessels of auricalc (a kind of brass) to draw wine with; 2 iron frying plates, 2 pot clips (to suspend pots over the fire), one flesh hook, one coal-rake, one wooden shovel [as used by bakers], one common shovel, one wheel-barrow, 3 cressets, one 'sae' or 'soe' [a tub with two projecting staves for carrying on a pole], two cans for milk, one scoop [a basin with a handle to ladle out water], two meat tubs, one pipe, and onetub in the pastry-house, one bolt cloth [for sifting flour], 9 tables or boards for dressing meat; two strainers, one iron tripod for frying, 7 iron bars for thebig tripod, one gallon measure made of wood for measuring honey.

In the Flesh Larder: 2 leaden cisterns, 9 steeping tubs, one flesh-axe, two dressing knives, two chopping knives, one slicing knife, one salt box, 23 dressing boards, 24 carcasses of oxen salted, one ox carcass powdered, one sheep powdered; 6 wooden chargers.

---

[22] *Rites ...* 93. *Fawden yetts* = folding doors.
[23] *Rites ...* 99, 280.
[24] *brandreth* = tripod placed on the hearth to carry a pot or frying pan.

In the Fish Larder: 5 steeping tubs, 3 other tubs, 2 steeping barrels, one barrel with fat, two barrels for keeping the fat, one barrel of salted salmon, one barrel of oil, one dressing knife, two chopping knives, one strainer or colander, one pair of weez [weights or wooden scales], with their weights, two dressing boards, two stockfish hammers, one great wooden charger, two wooden bowls.

Cellarer's Account Roll, 1438-9   *Dean and Chapter of Durham*

In the Store House: 1500 red herrings, 60 stock-fish, 330 dog-draves [cod].

In the Slaughter House: six fed oxen, one flesh-axe, one dressing-knife, 3 head-stalls, 5 stands, two cradles or crates, one pipe with a lock to keep fat in, two saes, one leaden vessel, one tub, one hollow vessel, two iron-forks, and two flaying-knives.

The Cellarer's Account Roll for 1477-8 shows a quern or hand-mill bought for the kitchen for 16d. [6.5p].

The Cellarer was responsible for seeing what flesh-meat was needed for the Kitchen each week, and what spices and 'other necessaries' were used both for the Prior's table and for the whole convent.[25] Spices included anise [aniseed from the middle east], cinnamon [mainly from Ceylon], cloves [from the Indian Ocean], confections, drage, galingale [from the East Indies],[26] ginger, liquorice, mace, nutmegs [from the far east], pepper, saffron [from Doncaster and Cambridge], and sugarplate [sugar from Cyprus], and in addition almonds [from the middle east], currants [from Greece], dates [from

---

[25] *Account Rolls, Volume 3*. The Preface (end of volume) has recipes and detailed lists of food bought by the Cellarer.

[26] *galingale*: the aromatic rhizome of East Asian plants of the genera *Alpinia* and *Kaempferia* used in cooking and herbal medicine. English galingale is a sedge with a root having similar properties.

North Africa], figs, hazel-nuts, prunes [possibly from France], raisins [from Spain], and onions. Mustard occurs infrequently, perhaps because it was produced on monastic property, although it occurs in the accounts for the cell on Holy Island. The word spice is now much restricted in use, but colloquially spice cake is plum or currant cake or bread. The 'other necessaries' included fish and fowl and many things besides. Olive oil was delivered in barrels.

The Cellarer's purchases during the week after Martinmas, 1333-4, are typical: one thousand eggs cost six shillings and nine pence [34p.]; a horse-load of whiting cost four shillings [20p.]; seven salmon, plaice and smelts cost four shillings and twopence [21p.]; pork and veal cost nine shillings and a half-penny [about 45p.]; seven sucking pigs, fourteen geese, and seventeen fowls cost seven shillings and fourpence halfpenny [about 37p.]; wild fowl cost three shillings 15p.]; butter and honey cost ten pence [4p.]; forty-eight fowls cost eight shillings [40p.]. Some provisions were delivered by priory tenants holding land by payment in kind.[27]

Dairy produce - milk and eggs - was a very important part of monastic diet, but only accounted for three per cent of the financial outlay. For the whole year 1333-4 no fewer than forty-four thousand one hundred and forty eggs were bought. Except in Lent, a monk might consume five eggs a day in various forms, and commonly had cheese at dinner time and often again at supper.

Bread made from wheat flour accounted for ten to fifteen per cent of the monastery's outlay on food.

Fish was eaten frequently. Some, known at 'stock fish', was dried by being exposed on stakes in the

Man beheading a cock: from a mid-12th century copy of Josephus: *Antiquities of the Jews,* from the Library of Durham Priory

Durham Dean & Chapter Library MS.BII.1,folio 237 verso.

sun, and had to be beaten with 'stock hammers' before cooking to make it palatable. Stock fish was probably kept or treated in the fish larder off the Great Kitchen. A great variety of fish was consumed, but in general the Cellarer chose white rather than fatty fish. Some sea fish came from Beadnall and some from the Tees. The bursar made regular payments for transporting barrels of herrings brought by packhorses from Newcastle,[28] but the Cellarer paid for the fish. About half was preserved by salting, smoking, drying or pickled in brine. 'Dog-draves' (a word unknown except at Durham), or cod and codling from the Dogger Bank, appear frequently in the accounts; there are also saithe, cod-like sea fish, also known as coalfish or coley. Nearly all was sea fish, and this became typical in all great households by the close of the middle ages. Eels were bought by the stick: a stick was twenty-five eels. Shell fish was eaten also, including mussels, limpets, oysters, and lobster.

[27] Reginald of Durham, *Libellus* ...Surtees Society 1, (1835), chapter 106, 238.
[28] Reginald of Durham, *Libellus* ...Surtees Society 1, (1835), chapter 106, 238.

Some fresh-water fish were used as special festival dishes served with cinnamon and ginger sauce, such as pike, which was eaten in winter, and burbot[29] or eel pout. Fresh water fish was kept until required in fish ponds or stews across the river in the Prior's manor of Crossgate.

There was a capon house and a goose house, but whether these were buildings or cages is unknown. Some chickens were kept alive in crates in the kitchen until killed fresh for the table.

Meals and serving

The life of a Benedictine monastery revolved (as it does today) round the services of the church; and meal times were arranged so as not to interfere with the pattern of daily worship. The eight daily offices or canonical 'hours' were divided into the night offices: *nocturns* (mattins) at midnight; *lauds* at dawn (in later times lauds followed mattins without a break); and the day hours: *prime* (before the daily meeting of the Chapter); the 'Little Hours': *terce* (at 9 a.m.); *sext* (at midday); *none* (at 3 p.m.); *vespers* (in the evening); and *compline* (the last office of the day, at bed time). In addition, as each monk was an ordained priest and expected to say mass daily, half said his mass at one of the many altars in the church and half attended the convent's high mass. In the later middle ages, when most of the monks would have risen at six, they would breakfast on bread and ale. When the dinner bell[30] rang at 11 o'clock, the monks left their work to wash their hands in running water at the lavatorium, a circular building housing the conduit in the cloister opposite the original refectory door.[31] On the cloister wall were cupboards, with traceried fronts to allow the circulation of air, where each monk had his clean towel and his own key.[32] After washing he could enter the refectory.

The tables were laid with table-cloths, salt cellars, and mazers or drinking bowls, kept in an aumbry or cupboard at the west end of the refectory. Each monk had his own mazer edged with silver double-gilt and his own knife. (Forks were unknown.) The high table was set also with a basin or ewer of latten (a kind of brass), shaped like a huntsman on horseback, used by the Prior or sub-Prior to wash his hands at table. Suspended here was an ancient bell, believed to have belonged to St Cuthbert,[33] which the novice master rang after each meal to tell one of the novices to say grace. After grace was said, a large mazer, called the Grace-cup (kept in a cupboard on the left of the refectory door), was sent round the tables. Meals were served by the yeomen of the kitchen.

The first dish at dinner was pottage, a kind of oatmeal soup with vegetables, and pieces of either fish or meat, followed by two further dishes of fish or meat. Supper was eaten in the afternoon. On special occasions pittances or extra delicacies were added, such as small birds, freshwater fish and game.

The daily allowance for a monk was a loaf, two justicias (half a gallon) of ale (known as the monks' justice), two portions of pulse or beans, and two commons of flesh or fish.

A choice between two dishes of cooked food was offered throughout the year; yet there was concern 'that the monks be not overtaken with indigestion'. Meals were taken in silence, except for Bible readings from the Old or New Testament in Latin from the refectory pulpit by a novice.

Who was served from the Great Kitchen?

Large quantities of food were served in the later middle ages. The number of monks varied, not counting those in the separate cells: thirty-three in 1448, later sixty-two; and the novices who always dined with their master in the refectory. Meals were taken also to other parts of the Priory. Some of the

---

[29] *burbot*: an eel-like flat-headed bearded fresh-water fish of the family *Zoarcidae*, with a slender body and dorsal and anal fins meeting to fuse with the tail.

[30] The bell hung east of the conduit door. *See* Rites ... 82.

[31] To the east of the present door. James Raine, *A Brief Account of Durham Cathedral, &c* (1833), 93, mentions the blocked doorway, no longer visible. The basin is now in the centre of the cloister garth.

[32] *Rites* ... 79.

[33] Reginald, *Libellus* ... 81, 168-72; 170 note; Prior Turgot (1087-1107) had this bell gold plated.

obedientiaries did not eat with the community as a rule, but had their meals served in their own exchequers: two certainly had this privilege, the Sacrist, whose exchequer lay off the north choir aisle of the church, and the Bursar, whose exchequer was in a stone building adjoining the coal garth near the Great Kitchen. Besides the Cellarer's exchequer, there were others. For example, the Chamberlain had his exchequer near the gateway into the South Bailey where his staff included a tailor and assistants to make clothes, table linen and bedding; the Terrar or Hostillar had his office just within the entrance to the Guest Hall; the exchequer of the Master of the Common House was in a wainscoted enclosure under the north end of the dormitory in the common house itself, the only place where a fire was always allowed under the Rule of St Benedict.

Hospitality was an important feature of monastic life, continuing in monasteries today, and guided in the Rule by Christ's words: 'I was a stranger and ye took me in'. The main fare for the Guest Hall, which often had many guests, was cooked and served from the Great Kitchen and the Hostillar had the help of four yeomen. He provided only wine for the strangers, certain luxury foods for the guests and their bed and table linen. All travellers of standing stayed there for several days, with attendants necessary in view of the dangers on the roads. The Guest Hall lay just to the south-west. Next to it was the Infirmary, which had similar provision from the Great Kitchen for its sick and aged inmates. It was reached through a passage between the great cellar and the common house (now the Treasury) beneath the dormitory.

The Prior lived in state as other noble lords: his household of twenty or more, often had in addition special guests, and included his esquires (young men sent from noble houses to learn etiquette), who had their own hall and who also had to be served from the Great Kitchen, using the connecting service passage.

Corrodians (pensioners) had meals taken to their own dwellings.

In addition there were many lay servants (conversi), to be fed, upwards of sixty in the mid-sixteenth century. Some of these were specifically connected with the work of the Great Kitchen and the provision of food. Among the valecti or upper servants was one in charge of the wine cellar, a cook or victualler, the cook of the lord Prior, a steward of catering, a baker, a brewer, and a cook of the flesh larder. Lower servants or grooms helped the cook, caterer, and Cellarer, and included also a fisher, seetherer (or boiler), slaughterman, and ale-drawer, besides those serving as baker and brewers. When any extra work was in hand, paid craftsmen who served on a daily basis had food provided. Women were employed on menial tasks such as drawing water, bringing in wood for the fires, dealing with the napery, and in laundering. We do not know where they ate: perhaps in the kitchen itself.

In the monastic Almonry, near the gateway from the outer court (now the College) into the Bailey, lived four aged women fed from the Prior's table, and here was the Almonry School (a free grammar school) whose boys had food from the novices' table served by the Clerk of the Covey. The modern visitor to the Great Kitchen enters from the south alley of the cloister, passing the covey hatches where two boys collected meals to take to their own refectory.

Besides those staying in the Guest House, with its three valecti and three grooms, sometimes this already great household was increased by special guests, some of whom brought their own servants and retinue.

Occasional royal visits to Durham involved the consumption of huge quantities of extra food. When Edward III and his Queen came in 1333-4 with their retinues, these included in one week, 31 salmon, 5 carcasses of veal, 192 pullets and two capons, 33 geese, two stones [12.7 kgms] of cheese, butter and kids. On such visits the guests might be served swans, which had been fattened at one of the Priory's swanneries such as that at Ferryhill. Robert de Graystanes tells us that the King was taking supper in the Prior's Chamber on the Friday in Easter week when Queen Philippa joined him after riding over from Knaresborough. Being weary, she went early to bed. Soon a monk asked to speak with the King, telling him that if any woman slept within the precincts of the Convent some dire mishap would befall them all. Alarmed at the prospect of offending St Cuthbert, the King sent servants to rouse the Queen, who fled from the Prior's Lodging, out through the great gate, down the Bailey, and to the Castle entrance where she begged lodging from her cousin, Bishop Beaumont, although he was in failing health. No harm befell either the Queen or the Convent.[34]

We have the impression of the Great Kitchen busy with numerous servants, each with a special job as part of an orderly and well-regulated programme: a master-piece of organisation.

Sources of supply

Lindisfarne and the Farne Islands were sources of food. Annually in the Bursar's account appear the expenses of two monks going to Holy Island for rabbits at Christmas. Wild duck was caught there by snaring. After Durham Priory established a cell on Inner Farne in 1255, the Farne Islands regularly supplied the mother house at Durham with porpoises and seals as special delicacies at festivals until the dissolution of the Priory. For example the Receiver's book for 1538 records:

> For one sea swine [porpoise] bought of the Master of Fayrne, on the 1st of September, 10 s.
> To John Mondey, for its carriage, 2s 4d.
> One sea calf [seal] bought of the Master of Fayrne, against the Festival of St Nicholas, 5s.
> To John Mondey for its carriage, 2s 4d.

Durham, like other monastic houses, grew its own fruit and vegetables. Across the river in Crossgate beside St Margaret's church the monastery had gardens and fishponds. On its estate at Ferryhill, swans were kept in a special house for fattening for the table when important guests were entertained. Pigeons could be had from the small dove cote[35] on the roof of the lavatorium; or from the large round dove cote by Ambling Barns (near the modern Durham School swimming baths).

On the peninsula the Cellarer had an orchard south of the great court, and another outside on the east facing river bank. He had permission to reach it by a special gate through the defence wall, reached by a path opposite the Great Gate, as a short cut to save the longer route by the Water Gate. In earlier years he was responsible for seeing the gate was built up if danger from Scottish attack was envisaged.

In the later middle ages, however, the consumption of fresh fruit and vegetables began to be considered a luxury.

Meat was apt to be regarded as an indulgence, and eaten only on special occasions. Otherwise, following the Rule of St Benedict, who declared that flesh meat must be eaten apart, it could be consumed in the *misericord*, or *solarium caritatis*, a special room or loft, at the west end of the refectory, intended as a dining room for aged monks or those with special dietary needs. Offal, however, could be eaten in the refectory itself.

Very weak ale or beer was the staple drink as the water supply was impure; and for this reason it was used in cooking. A popular dish was 'Numbles': sheep's entrails mixed with breadcrumbs and spices and cooked in ale.[36] (At Westminster every monk received a gallon of ale daily, and there were extra allowances, such as that to the precentor when he sang the long office of a feast day.) Durham Priory's gyle house[37] and brewhouse were in the lane immediately to the right within the gate from the South Bailey.

By the end of the middle ages wine was served on feast days which numbered about a hundred each year.

---

[34] *Hist.Dunelm. Scriptores Tres, Gaufridus de Coldingham, Robertus de Graystanes, et Willielmus de Chambre* [edited by J. Raine] Surtees Society 9 (1839). *Graystanes* cap. xlvij, 117.

[35] *Rites* ... 82.

[36] Numbles: compare the expression to 'eat humble pie'.

[37] *gyle house*: where gyle or wort was allowed to ferment for brewing.

Recipes

The cooks had to be versatile not only in cooking for the ordinary needs of the monastic household and the special guests.

Some of the recipes used for the dishes served sound unpalatable by modern taste. *Scutum de Braune* (shield of brawn) was named from the skin of a boar, raw or tanned, which was called a boar's shield. The shield was placed round the inside of a cylindrical mould, and the middle was filled with prepared meat and fat. Many hours boiling gelatinized the tough hide, making all edible.

The Hostillar offered delicacies to those in the Guest Hall. They included oysters, and fruit such as almonds, figs, raisins, walnuts, apples, pears, wardons, and cherries. Sometimes confectionery was provided: anise comfit; madryan (sugar carefully melted over the fire and poured out on a marble stone dusted with rice flour, and flavoured by adding rose, violets, gilly-flowers, or other flower petals); dragy (a comfit containing a seed or grain of spice); Gobet reall (a royal gobbet or titbit, made of sugar coloured with turnsole - a purple dye from southern Europe); pinyonade (a sweet made of sugar boiled with pine seeds, seasoned with ginger and mace, put into boxes with cloves stuck in); and charcedoyne (a preserve of the pulp of quinces). Blaunch powder (finely powdered white sugar with ginger) is mentioned also.

The Commoner, in charge of the common house beneath the dormitory where a fire was kept, was allowed wine, nuts and fruit for the occasional little celebrations allowed to individual monks on anniversaries and on the eight days before Christmas.

B. From the dissolution to circa 1840

When the Priory was dissolved in 1540, the Prior remained as the first Dean, and the twelve senior monks became the first canons of the Cathedral Chapter. They continued to live in community for a time, taking their meals together and served from the Great Kitchen, and sleeping in the dormitory, but with the change they could marry, and gradually set up their own households in the buildings around the outer court, now known as The College (Cathedral Close). William Todd, D.D., was appointed first prebendary of the fifth stall and was assigned the Cellarer's exchequer as his residence: the upper floor of the building west of the Great Kitchen.[38] For a time the minor canons continued to take their meals together and the refectory became the Petty Canons' Hall, or dining room for the minor canons who continued for a time to live as a community, and needed a kitchen. As in other monastic cathedrals refounded by Henry VIII, the draft statutes required the minor canons and lay clerks to live in community like members of a university college, and a college cook was to be appointed. The communal life faded out about 1600, and the building was converted into separate dwellings for those who remained unmarried. These became ruinous and derelict by the end of the Commonwealth, when all church property was confiscated. In 1663 Dean Sudbury converted the refectory into the present handsome library.

The Prior's Lodging had now become the Deanery, and the Great Kitchen was taken over exclusively to cook for the Deanery household and its guests, by continuing to use the connecting service passage. The post-Reformation Dean and Chapter continued to offer hospitality to strangers. The Cathedral Statutes of 1555 issued to Durham under Queen Mary lay down detailed requirements for the provision of hospitality. There was new work for the cook. Each year the Dean and each of the twelve major canons was to devote at least twenty-one consecutive days to maintaining a household in the College, attending the Cathedral services, and keeping 'more sumptuous entertainment than they are wont at the other periods of the year, giving meat to the choir and inviting the citizens or strangers, as becomes those who are given hospitality'. Notice of the period had to be given in advance, and no two hospitality

---

[38] *Rites ...* 99, 280.

residences might overlap. Any canon failing to keep his hospitality residence lost his income from the Cathedral for a year, unless provided with a dispensation from the Crown.

Those invited included other members of the Chapter, minor canons, the lay-clerks, King's Scholars with their headmaster, local tradesmen, tenants, the cathedral bedesmen and their wives, canons' housekeepers on board wages keeping the house aired and in order (when they were absent attending to duties elsewhere), cathedral servants (in the servants' hall), and occasional visiting gentry. The choristers and King's Scholars each read a part of Psalm 119 every day during the residence, just before the table cloth was removed; and for this each received one shilling [5p.] at the end of the residence. A Grace-cup of silver gilt (still in existence and occasionally used) was passed round to perform the same service as its monastic predecessor.

We hear of the verger on duty issuing an invitation to the residence dinner to any strangers noticed at Evensong. A delightful account has survived of the visit of three soldiers from Norwich, 'a Captain, a Lieutenant, and an Ancient' to Durham in 1634. They were noticed at the Cathedral service by Dean Hunt, who sent one of his 'Ambassadors' to invite them to a residence dinner in the Deanery. Dr Hunt walked and talked with them in his garden for half-an-hour until dinner was served. Venison and salmon were among other good things on the menu. After the meal a 'there came a young Scholler, and read a Chapter', one of the King's Scholars from the grammar school (Durham School), reminiscent of the duty of a medieval novice. There followed the 'cup of wine', doubtless the Grace cup. The Dean begged them to stay a week but they begged leave to continue their journey according to plan.[39]

The Dean and Chapter's cook was employed at different houses to cook residence dinners; and worked in the Dean's Kitchen when the duty fell to the Dean. In the mid-18th century the cook was John Thacker who found time to run cookery classes and to publish a cookery book:

ART of COOKERY. 199

To make a sweet Calf's Head Pye.
Paté d'une tête de Veau.

SPLIT, and wash the Head very clean, let it lie to foak in Water all Night; boil it pretty tender, let it lie to cool, cut it in Slices, feaſon it with Salt, Nutmeg, Cinnamon, Mace, and a little Pepper, all beat very fine; ſheet your Diſh with cold Paſte, lay in a Lare of Calf's Head, ſome Raiſons ſton'd, Currants dried and clean'd well; then lay in ſome more of the Head over that, with ſome Fruit over that as before; the Tongue being ſliced and put in with the reſt; keep this Order till it is all laid in; put in a little ſtrong Broth, lay Butter on the Top, lid it, and bake it; when it is baked, melt half a Pound of Butter, with half a Pint of White Wine, the Juice of a Seville Orange, and ſome Sugar; cut a Hole in the Lid of the Pye, and put it in; ſhake it all together, and ſend it up.

C 2   To

The Art of Cookery by John Thacker, 1758
"To Make a Sweet Calf's Head Pye"

The Art of Cookery containing above six hundred and fifty of the most approv'd receipts heretofore published ... also, a bill of fare for every month in the year... Being a book highly necessary for all families, having the grounds of cookery fully display'd therein.

By John Thacker, cook to the Honourable and Reverend the Dean and Chapter of Durham.[40]

---

[39] 'A relation of a short Survey of 26 Counties ... Observed in a Seven Weeks Journey begun at ... Norwich On Monday, August 11th, 1634, and ending at the same place, By a Captain, a Lieutenant, and an Ancient; all three of the military Company in Norwich. In *Reprints of Rare Tracts ...* [by] M.A. Richardson [from British Library Lansdowne Ms] (1848).

[40] Newcastle upon Tyne: printed by I. Thompson and Company (1758).

In the Preface, Thacker says: *At the Request of my Friends, especially my Scholars, I have publish'd this Book.* He includes 'A set of bills of fare for the Residence in the College of Durham, begun September 29th 1753.' The menus are rich and varied. There was no clear sequence of courses as is the custom today, when those present are each expected to take some of the dish offered: this dates from the early nineteenth century. As many as ten dishes were put on the table at once, and the guests helped themselves to what they fancied.[41]

The founding of the University brought about further changes. The number of canons or prebendaries was reduced from twelve to six, and the income which had supported them devoted to fund the new institution. Fewer canons' houses were needed. The Cellarer's office, the Loft and the south end of the dormitory, had become the house of the prebendary of the fifth stall, whose last incumbent was Canon Valerian Wellesley, brother of the Duke of Wellington.

C. 1840 - 1940

When Canon Wellesley died in 1848 the Dean and Chapter decided to remove his house from the south end of the dormitory;[42] It had been reached by a long flight of steps beside the west wall of the Cellarer's office which had been part of it, and it was demolished in 1849.[43] The south end of the ground floor is recorded as containing a stable in 1820. The demolition left the west side of the Great Kitchen exposed as it is today.

It must have been difficult to serve meals hot in the Deanery when they were cooked in the medieval kitchen. Latterly, the food was kept warm by using heated trolleys in the service passage. Within living memory[44] this passage was cleaned by throwing down buckets of water from the upper end, and swilling it down to the kitchen where a channel in the stone floor ran into a drain in the middle.[45]

In addition to the Deans' later use of the kitchen for domestic purposes, it was useful also for catering on special occasions when more meals were needed. The Dean and Chapter provided audit dinners for their tenants from the Durham district on rent days until the early twentieth century. After a period when these were held at a public house in New Elvet, that in 1902[46] was to be held in the dormitory with the catering done in the Great Kitchen 'provided Mrs Chapman submits a suitable tender'. The same arrangements were made in 1903.

A former dean is said to have shown his kitchen to a friend who remarked: 'What a fine chapel it would make' (as there was then no chapel in the Deanery). The dean replied: 'I hope that I shall never live to see such desecration'.[47]

The Great Kitchen was, however, destined for new uses. It was last used for domestic purposes by Dean Alington in 1940, when a small and more convenient kitchen was built adjacent to the dean's dining room at the south end of the Priors' Hall.

---

[41] Friends of Durham Cathedral, *Fifty-third Annual Report,* 1985-86, 20-24, P. Mussett, 'Cathedral catering'. Other material about the food cooked here will be found in a document of the 1770s in Northumberland Record Office.

[42] *Dean and Chapter Minutes*, Volume 3, 996.

[43] *Rites ...* 280. The roof line of these buildings was still visible in 1903.

[44] Information from the late Edward Clark, Head Verger of Durham Cathedral, who retired at Michaelmas 1967. (Friends of Durham Cathedral, *35th Annual Report*, 1967/1968.) He had worked at the Cathedral for more than forty years. His wife Vera was housekeeper at the Deanery.

[45] J.C. Wall, *Durham Cathedral* (1930), 169 is mistaken in stating that this was a medieval channel for blood from the slaughter house.

[46] *Durham Chapter Acts*, 1 Feb., 1902.

[47] J.C. Wall, *Durham Cathedral* (1930), 169-70.

'Groining of the Kitchen',1911 *W.S.Footitt,1911*. The Priory Kitchen adapted for Deanery use. Illustrated in G.W. Kitchen, *The Story of the Deanery,* (Durham), 1912

D. The 'Prior's Kitchen': 1951-1995

The Great Kitchen was renovated between 1949-51 for use as a document repository. Known as the Prior's Kitchen from 1951, it housed the vast collection of monastic archives dating from the eleventh century and the later records of the Dean and Chapter of Durham Cathedral, together with Bishopric documents and some other deposits. It was staffed by the Department of Palaeography and Diplomatic in the University of Durham.

The spits and other equipment in the fireplaces were stripped out, and bookcases occupied the central floor space. The remains of the fittings for the smoke-jack are visible, embedded in the masonry over the fireplace on the east side. The covey and cellars were used as document repair shops.

When the passage was demolished early in 1949 to make way for the Durham Light Infantry Memorial Garden the floor of a building, probably the earlier monastic kitchen, was uncovered to the east of the fourteenth-century (present) kitchen.[48]

During investigations beneath the floor of the old library in 1960-2, quantities of bones of cattle were discovered. They were all from young animals, mostly under six months old, a clear indication that the seventeenth-century canons lived mainly on veal. Although the majority were seventeenth century, a large second group was very much older, suggesting that material from an old midden had been deposited there after the Dissolution and before the rebuilding in the 1680s. This was confirmed by the presence of medieval pottery.

Excavations on the site of the cellarer's exchequer at the south end of the dormitory have revealed medieval kitchen debris which contained the remains of freshwater fish, especially perch, sheep and other animal bones.[49]

Further work on the Prior's Kitchen was carried out in 1969-71, when the plaster was removed from the interior walls, exposing the stonework and the relieving arches.

E. Modern use

The monastic documents and Dean and Chapter records were moved from the Great Kitchen to 5 The College in 1995; and the Bishopric and other documents were transferred to Durham University Library's Archives and Special Collections on Palace Green. Work began on the buildings to enable the SPCK Cathedral Bookshop to move from the dormitory undercroft in September 1997.

The Great Kitchen was opened officially as the new bookshop in December by Tony Blair, the Prime Minister.

I am indebted to Norman Emery, Roger Norris, Pat Mussett, and Martin Snape for their help in drawing my attention to material which I should otherwise have missed.

---

[48] Friends of Durham Cathedral, *Sixteenth Annual Report, 1948-9*, 12-15.
[49] Information from Norman Emery, Cathedral archaeologist.